Arabia Felix:

IMAGES OF YEMEN AND ITS PEOPLE

by Pascal Maréchaux

with 86 illustrations, 81 in color

Barron's
Woodbury, N.Y.

For Etienne Renaud

The author wishes to express his gratitude to Mme Dominique
Champault, Maître de Recherche at the C.N.R.S. (Musée de
l'Homme), for her invaluable assistance, especially in the preparation
of the captions to the colour plates.

First U.S. Edition 1980 by
Barron's Educational Series, Inc.
113 Crossways Park Drive
Woodbury, New York 11797

Translated from the French
Villages d'Arabie Heureuse
by Jane Brenton

All inquiries should be addressed to:
Barron's Educational Series, Inc.
113 Crossways Park Drive
Woodbury, New York 11797

International Standard Book No. 0-8120-5368-0

PRINTED IN SWITZERLAND
BOUND IN FRANCE

'If the water in a pool is not moving, it becomes stagnant and muddy, but if it stirs and flows, it becomes clear again; the same is true of a man on a journey.'

Muhammed Asad, *Le Chemin de la Mecque* (Fayard).

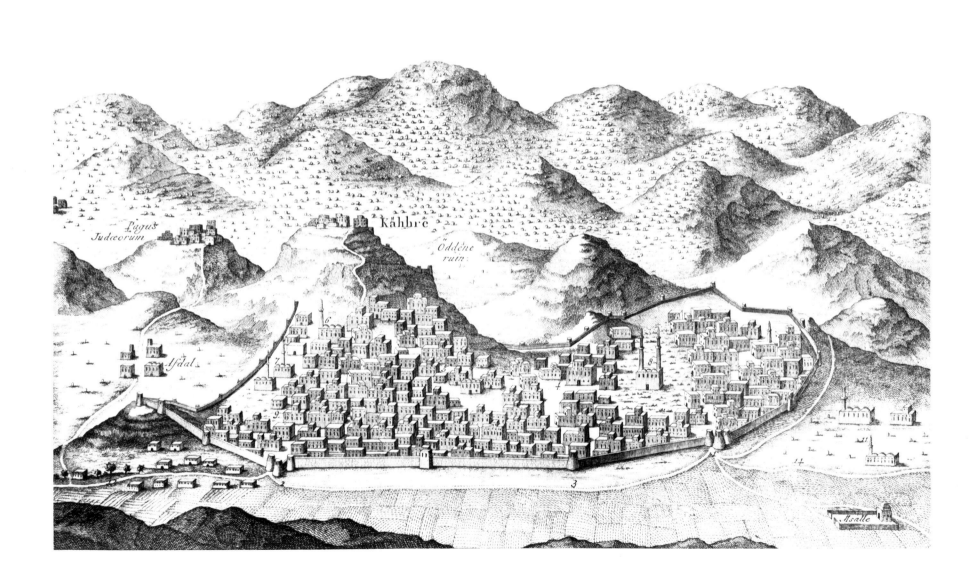

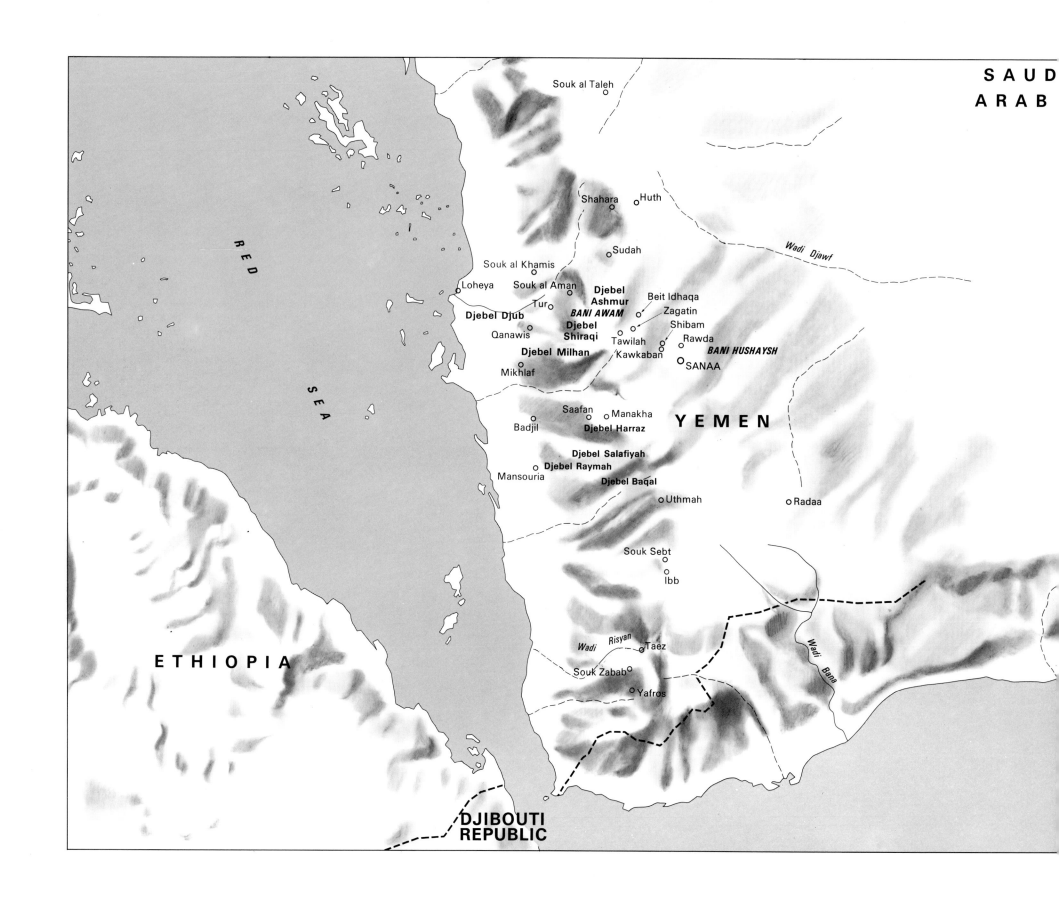

SAUD
ARAB

Souk al Taleh

RED

SEA

Shahara ○Huth

Sudah

Souk al Khamis
Loheya ○ Souk al Aman
Tur ○
Djebel Djub
Qanawis
Djebel Shiraqi
Djebel Milhan
Mikhlaf ○

Djebel Ashmur
BANI AWAM
Beit Idhaqa
Zagatin
Shibam
Tawilah Rawda
Kawkaban *BANI HUSHAYSH*
○SANAA

Saafan ○Manakha
Badjil **Djebel Harraz** **Y E M E N**

Djebel Salafiyah
○**Djebel Raymah**
Mansouria
Djebel Baqal
○Uthmah ○Radaa

Souk Sebt
○
Ibb

ETHIOPIA

Wadi Risyan ○Taez
Souk Zabab○
Wadi Bana
○Yafros

**DJIBOUTI
REPUBLIC**

Wadi Djawf

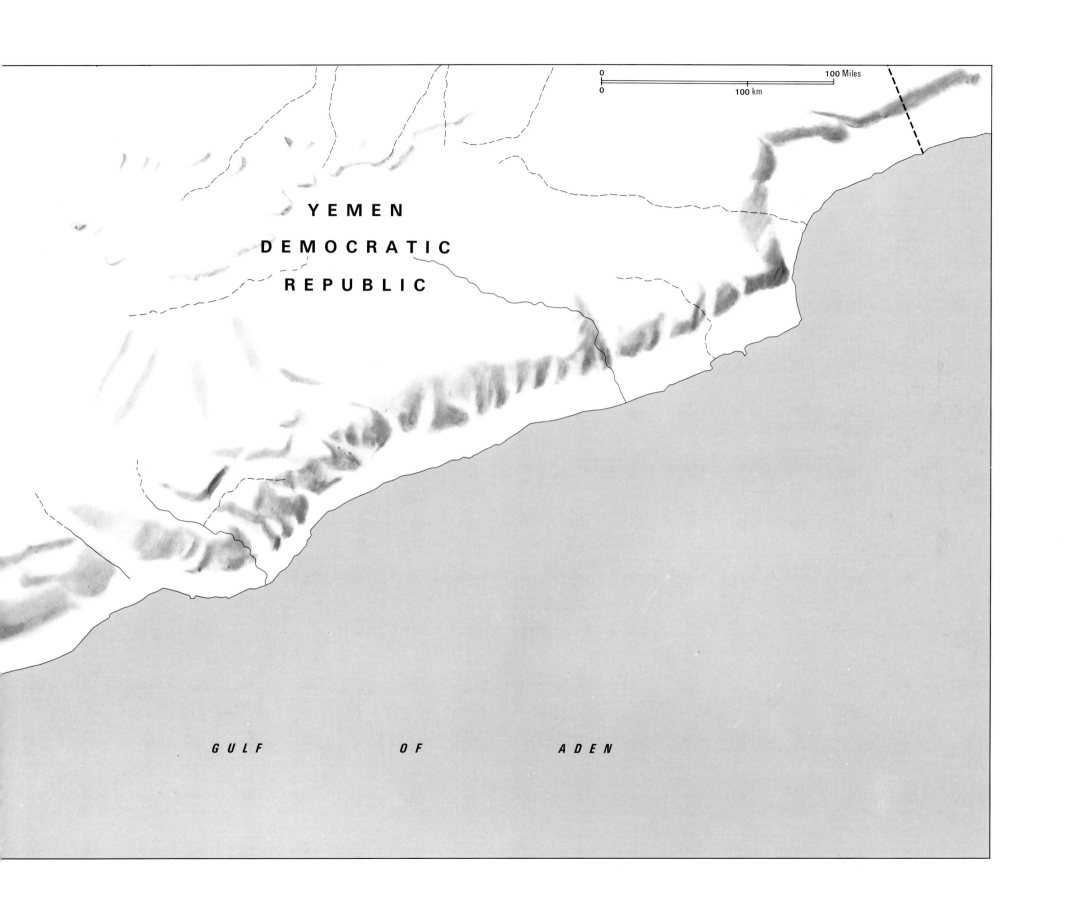

YEMEN

DEMOCRATIC

REPUBLIC

0

0

100 Miles

100 km

GULF   OF   ADEN

Djebel Milhan

The women have been up since first light and are busy preparing flat cakes of bread. The smoke rises slowly in the cool dawn air. It is six o'clock, and in the *djebels* (mountains) of the Yemen it is time for the first prayer of the day.

The mountains are wet from yesterday's rains and begin to glisten in the light – the monsoon from the Indian Ocean allows a variety of crops to flourish here. The ancients called the region Arabia Felix ('Happy Arabia'), because it is blessed with water, unlike the surrounding deserts of Arabia Petraea ('Rocky Arabia').

The fog that has crept up in the night from the coastal plain of the Tihama, by the Red Sea, starts to disperse. Sky and mountain. Mountain and sky. Nothing else. Vast.

Now the sun has swallowed up the last traces of concealing mist. Rocky spurs are revealed as villages, mountain slopes as amphitheatres tiered with broad terraces. Man's influence is everywhere. The reputation of this race of farmers and builders suddenly becomes a reality. Here, building is on the scale of the mountains themselves. Landscape and architecture are one and the same thing.

Djebel Salafiyah

I go to see the sheikh as soon as I arrive in the village. I am all alone and feel rather lost. He asks for a pass I don't have. I take out my photos and drawings, show him a letter of introduction; in no time it's all settled.

The next day, as I am about to leave, he even presses on me five silver dollars for my journey. It is a royal gift and one I can't refuse without causing offence.

Nothing seems to have changed since 1779, when Carsten Niebuhr reported how the local chiefs 'provided for the needs of travellers, and on their departure even offered them a sum of money to help them on their journey'. And in the next century, Botta, on an expedition for the Museum of Natural History in Paris, in 1837, noted that 'this generosity is not at all an individual characteristic; among the Arabs, hospitality to strangers has always been regarded as the prerogative of the sovereign', to the point, apparently, that Botta heard the local people being forbidden to accept anything from him, for any reason whatsoever, as the ruler would pay them for anything he took or any service they provided. This generosity in the end became a hindrance, because the merchants knew they would have difficulty in obtaining their money and therefore hid their goods rather than be left with nothing.

Beit Idhaqa

The mountain echoes to the crying of a child, the crowing of a cock and the braying of a donkey.

I scramble down to the *wadi*, or river. The path winds between coffee-shrubs, on through a village, skirting rocks and paved embankments, and passes near a spring, where a green leaf is delicately poised to catch the water.

In the shade of a big overhanging rock, a couple are weaving blankets of black goats' hair. The man passes the shuttle to his companion and sharply taps the thread into place. Farther down, where the fields broaden out, are two small stone houses: ten chicken, twenty goats, a woman and two children. The little girl stands in the open doorway shaking a gourd full of fresh milk. Inside the baby swings in a hammock, surrounded by flies. The father offers me the only egg in the house. No thank you. 'Shukran.' I go right down to the *wadi*, where a channel veers away carrying water to the crops – maize and a few banana trees. Monkeys stop drinking and chatter as they scramble back to their perches. Birds fly off, startled. A boy sways in the leafy stems of a tree. The path follows the dry river-bed, and soon pebbles give way to rocks. A snake slithers out like a red finger from under the stones. At the junction with another *wadi*, a few shacks stand empty, waiting for the crowds of the *souk*, or market, on Tuesday.

In the sticky midday heat, I climb to the village perched high on the ridge. Set there on the rocky crag it merges with its surroundings, making it hard to separate the natural from the man-made world. The houses are built close together, forming a solid wall. Their windows are edged with white: bold and imaginative patterns that stand out in the distance, designed apparently to attract the light and keep away the flies.

There is a low doorway, and often a second smaller doorway within it, so that you have to lower your head as you go in, possibly as a mark of humility and respect to the owner of the house. Inside, the stairway seems like a continuation of the path. It is unlit, and an enemy would have no easy task in launching an attack. The stairs lead through the various lower stories, used as store-rooms, past the women's and children's rooms, and thence to the calm of the *mafradj*, the reception room where the men sit together chewing *qat*, a plant with health-giving and euphoric properties.

The room is narrow, no more than ten feet wide, corresponding to the size of timber available in the region.

A toothless, white-bearded old man chops in a mortar the young shoots his tired jaws can no longer chew. Each with one cheek distended by its quid of leaves, the friends carefully select the most tender shoots, which they proceed to masticate, interminably.

At times some holy saying is muttered by one and taken up by the rest, spreading like a wave through the room. They sit there, side by side, sunk in the heavy fumes they exhale. A mouthful of cold water now and again, a jet of green saliva, and the ritual continues.

The windows are open to the mountain and the sky, where, down below, eagles are hovering.

Djebel Baqal

The path is narrow. It follows a well-worn track alongside terraces of guinea-corn (millet), sometimes joining up with the little irrigation channels that trap the rain water and carry it to stone cisterns. Projecting stones serve as steps between the terraces.

They become steeper and narrower, like a stairway where there is barely room to plant one coffee-shrub or one small tree of *qat* on each step. Down below are two minute figures of men, steering a plough or a harrow – impossible to tell which from here – along a narrow ribbon of ochre.

At intervals there are stone shelters, marking the way ahead. Not that you could lose your way. The direction to go is always upwards, climbing under the leaden sun. The light hangs down like a screen over the distant mountains.

The clouds gather with the approaching storm, and suddenly the skies open. In the darkness I run to the next shelter, my clothes steaming in the trembling air. Someone is there before me: he looks at me, astonished, from where he sits on a stone, his dripping donkey at his side, then smiles and offers me a piece of crumbling bread. The landscape reappears in gaps between the clouds. There's no reason to linger, so I walk on.

At dusk the village at last comes in sight, bringing with it the bliss of a scalding glass of tea and a cool evening breeze.

Tawilah

A face appears at an opening in the façade. 'Ahlan wa-sahlan.' ('You are with your family now, may your foot touch easy ground.') The door opens, a small boy appears and shows me the way. The stairs are uneven and dark and you need to feel your way up. Some of the steps have a small vertical slit in the wall beside them, letting in a piercing shaft of light. The women slide away, the man awaits me. I take off my shoes and go in. He takes my hand and touches it to his lips. I return the gesture. He is comfortably wrapped in blankets and takes down a goatskin for me, which he places round my shoulders. It's cold after the exertions of the climb. He serves me *qishr*, which is a brew of the outer husks of coffee beans, infused in boiling water and spiced with ginger. Twigs stuck in the neck of the jug act as a filter. In honour of the visitor, a girl runs to the chest and brings back a little sugar in her skirt.

The *Hadjdj*, so named because he has made the pilgrimage to Mecca, sits on the floor in the gloom, propped up by cushions. He is reading the Koran, his old pince-nez perched on his nose, and he is smoking. The room is filled with the soft murmur of the pipe that distils dreams and pleasures. Your head spins as you draw the smoke in and out. You put the mouthpiece to your lips, bite it gently, breathe very hard, release the pressure; heaviness and relaxation flood your body.

Uthmah

The guard sitting in the shadows signals me to go up. The landing is scattered with shoes. The door opens onto a spacious *mafradj*, filled with light and smoke. Four big pipes, rifles hanging on the wall, some coloured thermos flasks, a small desk: it is here that the sheikh dispenses justice. Elected by his kinsmen, it is his task to maintain law and order in these villages where daily life is still marked by fierce tribal divisions. The influence he wields is a function of his charisma and diplomacy, and the skill he has shown in reconciling opposing parties.

Ensconced in cushions in one corner of the room, one leg stretched out before him on the carpet, he invites me to take my place beside him. To do this, I have to run the gauntlet of a double row of inquiring eyes. The floor is strewn with branches of *qat*. The bubble of the *narghiles* resumes, and I become immersed in the proceedings.

The sheikh listens, selecting the best shoots of *qat* as he does so, and gives his reply without once raising his voice, merely speaking faster at times. He is the mediator. Everything is done through him. A man advances to the centre of the room, sits back on his heels, then prostrates himself, before presenting his petition. From the sheath of his *djambia* – the curved dagger worn by all the men – he takes a carefully folded sheet of paper. The secretary reads it, the sheikh signs it and throws it at the man's feet. The affair is closed.

Two plaintiffs take the central position. An old man, who has previously been silent, erupts into life, enacts anger, pretends outraged good faith, throws his turban on the floor, then sinks back into immobility. The sheikh whispers into his neighbour's ear.

The old man suddenly launches on another performance. He gesticulates, shouts himself hoarse and passes a crumpled scrap of paper forward to the sheikh, who takes it, examines it, tears it up and gives the pieces to his secretary to chew – which he does, and spits them out again dripping with green saliva. A third person joins the fray, amid shouts from all sides. Then the mood relaxes, calm and silence return. Individuals go up to the sheikh and address him politely. He in turn deliberates and writes his judgment, using the palm of his hand as a rest. His secretary reads the paper and then sticks it on the hook above his head, where the verdicts pile up, one on top of the other, until they fall to dust, the original disputes forgotten.

Shahara

Down below, a bridge spans a precipice. The path winds over the mountainside. In these steep and lonely places, it is easy to imagine how difficult it was for a central government to impose the rule of law and put down rebellious tribes clinging fiercely to their independence. A woman

toils up the mountain with a load of wood; a pair of horned cattle return from their day's work. Up on the pass, a cistern has been hewn out of the rock. Spiralling steps lead down to the water with its film of green on the surface. What would be a danger signal for me can be an indication of freshness for the Yemenites. Botta notes that they refuse to use standing water for their ritual ablutions unless it is covered by this weed.

The women are drawing water. Laughing young girls, with a shy, spontaneous charm, already women themselves, accompany their mothers. One girl stands bolt upright, using a cut-away gourd to fill the vessel already balanced on her head. Fetching water is a female duty, and in a family where several women share one husband and all the work between them, the senior wife will assign this task to the youngest or oldest among them.

There are a few pre-Islamic cisterns that have been in use since the Himyarite period, remarkable evidence of the technology used to control the water supply, which – together with the trade of the spice caravans – was the foundation of the prosperity of the ancient Arabia Felix. The first rupture of the dam at Mareb, the most famous of these hydraulic constructions, occurred in about A.D. 120, and brought about the collapse of the numerous small kingdoms that had flourished on the fringe of the desert for over ten centuries. Bilquis, Queen of Sheba, who is said to have visited Solomon, is one of the legendary figures of these vanished kingdoms.

Souk al Aman

The cows brought here the previous day have their throats slit and are hung on makeshift tripods and skinned. It's done very quickly. The men put their knives between their teeth and pull out the guts in handfuls. The long shadows cast by the dawn light fall on earth clotted with blood. A red pool oozes in rivulets beneath the tripod, and the dogs fight. When animals are killed for sacrifice, every morsel of meat is divided into as many portions as there are participants in the drama, each being allotted his own pile of tripe, fat, liver, bones and skin. But today the meat is for anyone who wants it. The kites swoop over the carnage, the crowds flock around the slaughterers. The narrow street is jammed. On foot, two to a donkey, alone or in groups, they have come for meat, which they eat very rarely except on feast days and at weddings.

In the streets the bargaining and selling take their course. Suddenly a shot is heard; the crowd stops to listen, taken by surprise. The *dawshan* shouts an announcement. The uproar resumes, intensified. The *dawshan*, or story-teller, does not belong to the village. He is at the very bottom of the social scale and lives alone in a tent. But like the *muezzin*, or master of ceremonies, who occupies a similar position, he is at the centre of all festivities. The sheikh stands with a number of *djambias* in his hand, pressed by people demanding justice. When a dispute arises between two men, each gives his *djambia* to the sheikh, symbolically asking him to defend his interests. By handing over his weapon, a man implies that he will not take the law into his own hands, and he pledges his honour to abide by the verdict.

Farther on is the *qat* market. The merchants sell their day's pickings in bundles tied with banana stalks. *Qat* has immediate cash value and is tending to replace coffee, which is a less profitable crop and harder to grow. Trade in *qat* puts large sums of money into circulation through-out the country, enriching the growers directly, without the intervention of middle-men. The leaves need to be used fresh and are impossible to store.

Ibb

Between two stalls in the *souk* is the entrance to the great mosque. Noise and turmoil give way to peace and silence, broken only by the flapping wings of birds nesting in the panelled ceiling.

Barefoot, I walk over the warm flagstones to the shadow of the columns, where two old *qadis* are reading the Koran, mumbling in their beards. The *qadis*, or jurists, together with the *ulemas*, or scholars, make up a caste, based on the mosque, which traditionally performs certain administrative functions in the community. Islam may preach equality, but in practice there is a strict social hierarchy, based on profession, with the *sayyeds*, or descendants of the Prophet, at the top.

Two or three steps open into a passage over the sunken street, an archway leads to the minaret and thence to the area set aside for ritual washing. A few students live over the portico around the courtyard. Adjoining the school is a hospice for the blind – the 'clear-sighted' as they are called here.

It is time for the second prayer of the day. The men arrive in a group. To perform their ablutions, each man goes separately into a recess formed by low stone walls. The light reflects on the white surfaces, polished smooth with use. Now in the little lime-washed room, they face the *mihrab*, the niche used to show the direction of Mecca, and pray in unison, performing the ritual gestures. The wood-grain shows through the rendering on the walls. The only ornament is an old image of the Ka'aba, the sacred building at Mecca.

The stonework is undecorated except for its white colour – once regarded as sacred and used exclusively in the mosques. Yemenite mosques are restrained and simple, among the most austerely beautiful in the Islamic world. A square courtyard surrounded by flat-roofed arcades. Here the children come to stumble through the *suras* of the Koran under the strict eye of their teacher. Islam governs every aspect of daily life: the five prayers, the status of women, the patriarchal family, taxes, laws. It is the guiding principle from which all else follows. The country was, after all, converted to the faith during

the lifetime of the prophet Mohammed, who sent his tribes out to conquer the world as far as Andalusia and distant Transoxiania.

Here in the south of the country, and in the Tihama, the Shafite school of the Sunni sect is dominant, while the peoples of the high plateaus in the north are Zaydis of the Shia persuasion.

Taez

It is Ramadan. A sleepy afternoon, with only children in sight.

The men will soon be awake. Siesta-time is over, and the street comes slowly back to life. At the *funduq*, or hotel, meals are feverishly prepared. The food is served. The guests sit facing their steaming plates, but no one makes a move. At last the cannon booms out its signal, and the whole town begins to eat. It is sunset.

If you are travelling when the long-awaited hour arrives, your companion will take a few dates from his pocket to break his fast; this is the *iftar*.

Tur

The heat is fearsome, the humidity stifling. The mountains appear very distant, in my imagination like another world. The gap between the Arabian peninsula and the African continent, marked by the Red Sea, is a geograph-ical division that is contradicted by a host of details: the huts are the same here as there, the costumes and people are similar, and there is much evidence of cross-breeding, from the days of the Ethiopian invasions and in the present.

A tall tree stands at the entrance to the *souk* of Al Khamis, so called because it is held on Thursdays.

Each street of the *souk* has its own speciality: hats, pottery, sandals, cloth, herbs and medicinal powders, all laid out in profusion; baskets made of the hide of cows and dromedaries. All these things blur into the colour of the sand, interspersed with the white splashes of the costumes.

Business is conducted in an undertone. An old man strokes his beard, his questioner takes out a few bank-notes, which are refused, and the bargaining goes on. The fat of the sheep's rump must be felt, the cow prodded and poked, the dromedary's teeth inspected.

A woman clutches her young goat against her like a babe in arms. The barber has set up his stall in the shade and is shaving heads and letting blood, applying hollow horns to the skin. A fly settles insolently on a client's nose.

The barber, who also performs circumcisions, belongs to a despised class. Tradesmen here are governed by a particularly rigid hierarchy based on ancient notions of purity. Butchers, cobblers, tanners, dyers and weavers are held in low esteem, as are blacksmiths, who are felt to be in collusion with the evil spirits of fire.

The late shoppers are still arriving as others are ready to leave, their turbans filled with the day's purchases.

Loheya

Sleeping on a rope bed under the open sky, you wake with the sun. Behind a few scattered palm trees, the sand dunes mark the beginning of the desert, stretching into the distance as far as the sea. A string of dromedaries moves slowly across it, tiny against the vast expanse; patches of salt glisten, sometimes lying smoothly in sheets, sometimes piled up in rough scales.

Everything submits to the relentless heat. Beyond the desert lies Loheya ('the end of the world'), isolated, its air laden with moisture.

The ruined town is a desolate place. The Turks departed, leaving amid the huts a large mosque with cupolas, also a fort on the hill, where a large garrison was once stationed.

White houses, with collapsed lattice-work balconies, still stand, their tacky façades crumbling, haunted by the musty smells of the vanished life of the harems. A ramshackle hut bleaches on the beach. It marks the entrance to the harbour and houses two officials, who wait there every day for the afternoon's delivery of *qat*.

All along the coast a fringe of green pushes out into the waves. Two white sails appear on the horizon, poised between sky and sea. A stir of anticipation arouses the harbour from its customary torpor. The wind swells the triangles of sail, and the gulls flap away. The coast has a gently sloping shelf, permitting only the traditional shallow-draughted boats to approach the shore.

The *sambuks* are bringing bales of Indian tobacco from Djibouti. They moor in the shallows. Porters wade, up to their chests in water, to unload the cargo. They return, bent under their burdens, bodies glistening with sweat, wet loincloths sticking to their skin. Occasionally they stop and an old negro serves them tea, which tastes brackish in spite of the sugar.

Right next to some abandoned hulks, wrecks of long ago, a boat is being refitted, its sleek hull propped up on stilts waiting to be caulked.

Later the fishermen return, having been out since dawn. Most of them have boats with engines, but even last year there were still a few who put to sea on rafts made of tree trunks. Sometimes the catch includes rays and small sharks. Two of the men, oars over one shoulder, unload a full basket onto the shore, while others bring in the nets that need to be mended before the next trip; handfuls of polyps or pierced shellfish serve as weights. Farther along the coast, the fishermen put out drag-nets from the shore and catch shoals of little fish, which are spread out in the sun before being rudimentarily salted and sent off to the markets of the interior. There is a new burst of activity in the *souk* with the prospect of the next meal, as the fishermen return. The bigger fish are filleted and strung onto the stems of palm leaves.

An old woman goes from one stall to the next, begging or filching a few little fish. Dozens of starving cats fight over the guts, which are already swarming with flies.

In the shade of the tea houses, the domino players while away the hours over patterns of black and white rectangles.

You leave the town behind and the desert claims you again, astonishing in its variety: patches of cracked mud, then sheets of salt; now and then, thorn bushes and clumps of harvested guinea-corn, holding back the sand; the dunes cast shadows, shifted by the wind so that they assume women's forms; a mosque and its tiny minaret overlook a basin of water and salt, its surface split with fissures. A donkey waits outside the doorway for his master to finish his prayers and return home with his load of salt. The white deposits gleam strangely against the dull shades of ochre. As though in sympathy with the weird configurations of the foaming earth, the far-away huts huddle together like a series of interlinked mounds.

Qanawis

In the sun-soaked plain, a few palm trees and some fields signal the proximity of the next village: straw huts with conical roofs cluster together inside palisades of thorn bushes and plaited rope.

Each compound contains one or more huts belonging to members of the same family, the number depending on the size and importance of the family. There is a paved area in front of the doorway where the rope beds, or *angarebs*, are placed in the evening: the air circulating through the branches and around the netting of the beds out here makes it easier to sleep in the heavy atmosphere.

The roofs are held in place by a fine net of plaited straw, and on the inside are caked with mud, on which the women paint simple geometrical and figurative designs, and fashion shelves to hold their prized enamelled plates.

On the outskirts of the village is the well, set on a mound in open ground; when it was originally dug, the displaced earth was used to make a slope, so that it would be easier for men and beasts to drag the heavy water buckets up to the well. The people take it in turns to draw water, bringing pulley and rope, vessels and animals. The pulley is fastened to the trunk of a palm tree; the notch becomes deeper every day as the cord rubs against it in the course of its slow ascent, to the accompanying splash of water from the overflowing bucket, which is finally emptied into troughs set flush into the ground or directly into oblong-shaped vessels.

The empty bucket falls back into the darkness and the rope runs freely over the pulley. Once the bucket is down, someone fastens the end of the rope to a donkey or ties it round himself, with the help of others. The women and children take hold and edge back from the well, pulling on the lengthening rope, in a formal ballet that is enacted over and over again.

The women wear a type of loose robe that is no more substantial than pockets of air held in place by thin veils of brilliant colour – red, black, orange – which ripple with the sheen of their skin as they move.

Sanaa

We're on the road. On the seat next to the driver is a turban overflowing with banknotes, to be given to the families of Bani Hadjadj whose menfolk have gone to work in Saudi Arabia. There's a lot of money in circulation in the Yemen, too much for prices to remain stable, not enough for everyone to be rich. Sanaa is full of money. Outside the bank a man is carrying wads of banknotes in his *futa*, or kerchief. Inside, the women clerks, veiled and dressed from head to foot in black, are rapidly counting piles of currency in vast coffers. For good or ill, the *souk* has succumbed to the brash charms of modern life. Radios are decorated with baubles and gold braid, cars are upholstered in fake fur, shops decked with trash, and the taxis flaunt brightly coloured electric light bulbs on top of their radio aerials – which

must be a good six feet long. Workmen, the mouthpiece of a *narghile* poking out from between their jacket and shirt, fabricate buckets and shoes out of old car tyres. The blacksmiths use scrap from old cars. The big hunks of metal swing through the air and are crushed on the red-hot iron, spewing out a stream of ashes and sparks. The men time the pace of their work and their breathing to the rhythm of holy chants. A cheapjack is wearing, one on top of the other, the jackets he is selling at give-away prices. Everything is changing too fast. Television aerials have sprouted on every row of houses; yet there was an eclipse of the moon the other night, and in the streets and at all the crossroads, bonfires were lit to exorcise the evil spirits of the darkness.

In the rubbish-strewn street there are piles of old tin cans, empty plastic bottles rolling about underfoot, evidence of the new eating habits under whose detritus the town is drowning – for the old habit of throwing everything into the street has persisted. But the mounting level of pollution arouses only indifference. After dark, the streets are peopled with shadowy figures, bent over their brooms: these are the *akhdams*. Remnants of conquered peoples, descendants of slaves brought from Africa, they move with the harvests, social pariahs, whose lot it is to perform the most menial tasks. Seeing them, one is forcibly reminded of the rigid hierarchy that divides Yemenite society into separate castes, in which inter-marriage is impossible. However, these distinctions, which are particularly marked among the northern tribes, are gradually becoming blurred in the towns, where a new middle class is beginning to emerge.

Saafan

Thursday's *souk*. At the front of a stall, a boy of scarcely twelve years old is engaged in a heated discussion with a customer. He is in charge of the shop, and I suspect he will have the last word in the argument. How could anyone contemplate leaving the running of a business to a child? Yet here it is nothing unusual, responsibilities are acquired early in life. I've seen children carrying rifles bigger than themselves. They play their part in all the daily tasks, the girls stay at their mother's side, helping in the kitchen and in the fields, and the boys accompany their fathers everywhere, even to *qat*-smoking sessions. I've seen them with fetters on their ankles – is it that they have committed some truly heinous crime, or have their fathers asked for them to be dealt with in this fashion? They take on responsibilities in childhood, and when they cease to be children they become adults. Adolescence is a meaningless concept here. Once a boy is circumcised he is given his *djambia*, a young girl is given her veil, and with them they acquire a clearly defined status in society. Can it be this security, this repressive yet liberating system, that gives the girls their confident bearing and laughing assurance?

Djebel Ashmur

The drum-beats mingle with the gun-shots and echo through the valley, reaching me as a series of muffled thuds.

Laden jeeps arrive, with men hanging on to the running-boards. From outside the chosen area – a small mountain pass – the warriors march downhill in closed ranks, guns on their shoulders, singing and shouting at the tops of their voices, holding hands, and brandishing their *djambias*. Those already there have gathered in a semi-circle along the large terrace overlooking the open field that has been transformed for the day into a forum. They stand watching the procession, musicians at its head. As they await the *amil*, or district officer, the dancers increase their tempo, raising clouds of dust. The drum and the *mismar*, a short, reedy flute, accompany them. The flautist's puffed-out cheeks are bound with a leather strap.

Soon the dancers brandishing their daggers have fallen back into a circle, leaving in the middle two virtuosi, who enact an extraordinary duel.

Groups from neighbouring villages arrive to swell the crowds. Today is the appointed day for the election of representatives of the Co-operative Development Union, which has recently been set up by the government.

The *amil* is the local administrator, whose job it is to implement the decisions of the central authorities. He arrives at last and takes his place on the terrace wall, a veritable tribune set above the tumult of the crowd. He has barely begun to speak when he is interrupted by a quarrel that breaks out in the audience. Two men hurl insults at each other and exchange blows. Their friends join in. The confusion is such that it takes much time and patience to separate them and stop the violence.

Finally the speech is started again, but its first words arouse a cry of indignation; one group makes as if to leave in disgust, others try to restrain them and fire shots in the air to make themselves heard. The most determined refuse to be deflected, and leave in a fury.

The *amil* meanwhile steps back to confer briefly with his advisers and his secretary to decide how to proceed. Order is eventually restored and the session begins in earnest.

Once all the facts have been established, each village forms a small committee to debate its choice, then returns to the assembly to elect representatives. The *amil* notes the names of those elected by a show of hands.

The days of the *imams* may be gone, but resistance to central government is very much alive – as this meeting shows. The problem is to impose an administrative hierarchy, while each individual still believes he has the right to go direct to the highest authority. He is accustomed to speaking face to face with his master. In the old days he could have gone straight to the *imam* to discuss the least little problem. President Al Hamdi, assassinated in October 1977, kept up the tradition, and every Friday used to open his doors to plaintiffs of all kinds and descriptions.

As the assembly draws to a close, one of the leading sheikhs invites me to lunch with him.

The women of the household are busy making preparations, helped by neighbours. They started work before sunrise. Before bread can be made, the grain must be ground. The woman and child talk as they turn the millstone. A paraffin lamp lights the scene. A beam of light falls intermittently between the moving figures and picks out the powdery grains. A hand moves into the light and back into the shadow with each revolution. On the backs of the hands is a fine black tracery, painted with antimony; palms and fingers are dyed with henna.

The fire roars under the *tannurs*, or ovens, in the stifling, smoky half-light. The flames lick the blackened stone dishes. The women take them firmly in their hands, without burning themselves, and place them on the embers to one side. One takes a ball of dough, spreads it flat on a round, floured pad, and bangs it down on the cylindrical surface of the stove; then, swiftly, with the tips of her fingers, just as it is about to fall in the fire, retrieves it and holds it up, golden, fluffy and crackling. The floor of the *mafradj* is spread with a feast. We have *bint al sahn*, hot flaky pastry with honey, *shafut*, made of bread and buttermilk, and *houlba*, a mixture of powdered fenugreek and water. For special occasions a whole sheep may be served, golden, coiled in a platter, stuffed with rice, hard-boiled eggs, pepper and raisins. Today the master of the house is sharing a simple mutton stew with his guests. The assembled company eats very fast, almost in silence, each using his right hand, because the left is regarded as unclean; later they will wash, before drinking tea and smoking *qat*.

Now, ensconced in cushions on the floor, each individual can enjoy the pleasures of *qat*, and the shared solitude, without feeling the company of the others as an intrusion.

The women eat the left-overs from the meal.

Djebel Shiraqi

It's time to leave the people who have given me a bed for the night, and with whom I've shared bread dipped in melted butter. Time to start walking before the full heat of the day. The sun is already shining down over Djebel Shiraqi – the mountains are like a sundial, each one has its hour. And each hour has its activity.

The mountain path is steep. A peasant is holding his cow back by the tail; it's a grey animal with spreading flat feet like floppy sandals. Bales of grass are being transported uphill: they are carried by women. Donkeys are picking their way down the mountain: they are ridden by men. Each village on the road is a veritable fortress. What better refuge than these mountains in the days of civil wars and the Turkish invasions?

In troubled times, the Zaydi *imams* used to withdraw to the security of these djebels. Although their period of rule was interrupted, there were in all sixty-six *imams*, who reigned as spiritual and temporal rulers, from the foundation of the dynasty in the ninth century by the great-grandson of Ali, brother-in-law of the Prophet, right up to 1962.

The house near the *souk* is small and shabby. The man conducts me there, having offered me hospitality. A pregnant woman, another who is older, a few children – they offer me their only bed, which I know I am meant to accept. They will sleep all together in a little side room. I feel embarrassed, the children look ill. Round their necks they wear little leather pouches containing magic verses, and round their wrists pieces of wool or strips of cloth, but these don't seem to have been very successful in keeping them healthy. The scar the man has between his eyes is the result of a burn inflicted to drive away sickness. He is affectionate to his children, but I know very well that he spends more on his daily ration of *qat* than he does on food for his family.

Wadi Risyan

The *wadi* flows all the year round, nature is generous. Each year four harvests can be gathered, but the land doesn't belong to the peasants, who keep only a third of the produce. Four landlords own all the fields between them, and agree among themselves how to distribute the water, vital for the soil to remain fertile. One of them, who married his sister to a landowner, and then killed him, has almost total control over the peasants.

Bani Hushaysh

The climate here is such that, in one day, it is possible to see all the activities of the farming year. There are women tipping loads of manure onto the fields. They wear shawls and brightly coloured dresses. Curious yet shy, they peep out at you, giggle and run away. The ploughman goads his team, one foot on the plough, pressing the share deep into the earth. Behind him, his wife, hat in hand, is sowing seed. At the back, a gaggle of children are strung out in a line, kicking earth back over the furrow and picking out the old roots. The people work hard, but find time to laugh.

Back at the village they are threshing corn on a sloping rock face. Shoulder to shoulder, the donkeys circle round, trampling stalks and ears of grain underfoot and dragging a heavy stone. To one side, the men are separating the corn from the chaff, aided by the wind. It's hot, and the dust sticks to their sweaty faces.

Down below, the vines in their stone-walled enclosures are sprinkled with soil: the light dust fills the air before it flies away. Perched on a wooden hut, a boy waves a branch to chase away greedy birds.

On the other side of the hill, a ploughman stands on a plank studded with nails, one hand clutching the cow's tail, the other holding the whip and the reins of the yoke, as he breaks down the big clods of earth. At the edge of the field, his wife is fashioning little plaits of lucerne and millet straw; at the end of each furrow she gives them to the animals, who like the lucerne and so eat the straw they

The engravings illustrating the first part of this book are taken from *Voyage en Arabie Heureuse* by Carsten Niebuhr, published in Paris in 1779.

would otherwise refuse. Fed like this throughout the day, the cows yield a good supply of milk.

The peasants summon me from a distance with a gesture that speaks volumes: the long journey ahead, the approaching dusk, and an invitation to stay with them until morning.

With its stones left loose on the top, the house looks like a ruin. It is nothing of the sort. If it were ever completed it would be a dead thing, incapable of growing; that would be both a bad omen and an insult to God, who alone can create anything finished or perfect. With these precariously balanced stones up above, a woman alone in the house can threaten any intruder who comes to disturb her peace. On the corners of the house, horns are fixed to the walls and are supposed to have the power of warding off the evil eye and protecting the house from evil spirits.

Wadi Djawf

In the eastern region, tribal opposition to the central authority is such that the government will not guarantee your safety. Foreigners have been kidnapped and held to ransom. My curiosity is sharpened by the sense of something forbidden, and I take advantage of the kindness of a local sheikh, Abdallah Ibn Yahya, to go deeper into the Djawf. His Kalashnikov always at his side, two clips of cartridges on his belt, he leads me across the difficult terrain. There are few villages, and the trees are stunted.

On a lonely outcrop of rock are a few houses where we can rest for a while. The walls are made of layers of earth piled one on top of the other, like a continuation of the strata of the rock face itself; you can still see the handprints of the builders. The method used is for one man to stand on top of the half-built wall, shaping and smoothing the clods of moist earth that are handed up to him by his two helpers. The layers turn upwards at the corners,

echoing the uneven row of stones at the base that serves as the foundation, and making the structure as a whole more resistant to the wind.

In the shade of the largest of the houses, some of the men are sitting in a ring waiting for their leader; others, their rifles slung over their backs, shift their weight from one leg to the other, resting. Their skin is a warm amber, the colour of peeled black grapes. Abdallah greets them, they kiss, nose to nose. Beyond the village, the women are washing clothes, wearing indigo veils with heavy silver clasps. The well is always situated outside the village. No one is allowed to live there. It belongs to everyone and is available for any passing Bedouin to water his animals.

Through the thick air, two cars are seen in silhouette; the *caïd* (leader) of the Djawf is here. A serious matter has arisen: a man has been killed on the borders of his tribal territory. Honour must be satisfied, blood shed in exchange for blood, according to the tribal code. They talk heatedly, then disappear. I don't know where to. Only the young children are left behind, asking me questions. My presence hinders them, a stranger is in their way, yet, faithful to the desert law of hospitality, the *caïd* accepts me as though his prestige depended upon it. He takes advantage of my presence to show that he knows how to conduct himself with foreigners, saying 'Please' and 'Thank you' in English, and makes it known that I have come at his request to photograph him in the company of his men. Generously, demonstrating his power, he entrusts me to the protection of four armed men, who are to take me to see the Himyarite ruins at Maïn. 'It's so old, so old', they say, wrinkling their brows and pursing their lips.

We are back in the desert, that universe of sand, unruffled by man's presence, that closes over our footsteps, serene and perfect. We stop at a dried-up *wadi*. The driver makes a hollow in the sand and water seeps into it; a few twigs are gathered from round about, and soon flames are licking at the tea-can.

Illustrations

This material was collected in the Yemen, which has a population of about five million in an area of some 76,000 square miles; it does not cover the Yemen Democratic Republic, which has a population of about one and a half million in an area of 112,000 square miles.

1   *This stone bridge is at an altitude of about 10,000 feet and links Shahara with the neighbouring mountain. The village of Shahara was one of the strongholds occupied by the* imams *during the Turkish invasions.*

2   *Djebel Raymah. Houses are often built on the mountain top, partly for defence, partly to free the fertile ground for the cultivation of crops.*

3   *Djebel Milhan. The regular rainfall makes it possible to grow cereals, coffee and* qat *on the terraced mountain slopes.*

4 and 5   *Djebel Raymah and Beit Idhaqa. The smoke rises slowly in the cool early morning air. At dawn, the women knead the dough and light the ovens to cook cakes of millet bread, which form the basis of the first, and most substantial, meal of the day.*

6   *Djebel Milhan. The technique of growing crops on terraces has been perfected as the result of a tradition going back over a thousand years. It is said that the practice spread from the Yemen to the French province of the Ardèche at the time of the Moorish invasions.*

7   *Coffee is harvested at various stages of maturity and is spread on the flat roofs to dry in the sun.*

8 and 9   *Bani Hushaysh. Threshing the grain. A team of donkeys or zebus (small oxen) tread the harvest, pulling a block of stone, or* madjarr. *The trampled straw is carefully collected, to be used either as animal feed or, mixed with cow dung, as fuel, or again, mixed with mud to build walls. The threshing floors are often collectively owned. An old woman spends the night in a nearby hut to guard the harvest. A full threshing floor is regarded as a sacred place, presided over by the* baraka; *empty, it is a place where it is better not to linger.*

10   *Bani Hushaysh. The climate is such that, in one day, it is possible to see all the activities of the farming year. Ploughing, harrowing, rolling and sowing take place concurrently, and any animal that happens to be available is pressed into service: donkeys, zebus or dromedaries. The harrow is reversible: one side is studded with spikes and used to break up the big clods of earth; the other side is smooth and acts like a roller.*

11   *Uthmah. Return from the fields.*

12   *Djebel Salafiyah. Much maintenance work needs to be done on the terraces. Every time it rains, the walls need to be repaired, and each year the soil washed down into the valley has to be carried up again.*

13   *Ploughing is done across the furrows left from the previous year; manure is dug in periodically to enrich the soil.*

14 and 15   *The village of Shibam looks out over a large fertile plain. Behind it is a steep rock face, at the top of which stands the village of Kawkaban. It is common for a trading post in the valley to be associated in this way with a well-defended mountain village or fortress; Thula and Kohlan are other examples.*

16   *Shahara. The only source of water on the high plateaus, today, as in the past, is the cistern in which rain water is collected. These cisterns are maintained collectively. They are usually covered in weed, which is regarded as a good omen if it is green, and is said to bring prosperity.*

17   *Details of the stonework of the cisterns.*

18 and 19   Sudah. The black robe, or sharshaf, worn by these women is a recent fashion borrowed from Egypt.

20 and 21   The mosque at Yafros possesses a small aqueduct which carries water to the various washing areas. The stone plugs set at water level are designed to let out the clean water on the surface during ritual purifications. The entrance to the village is by means of a tunnel underneath the courtyard of the mosque; the ventilation shafts can also be used to prevent unwelcome visitors from gaining access. The mosque is open to children; boys are actively welcomed, girls tolerated.

22 and 23   Ibb. The lectern, or koursi, is used for ease of reading and to preserve the purity of the sacred book. The ritual movements of the prayers are strictly laid down, even to the position of the feet. Certain differences in the gestures of the arms enable one to distinguish between the Shafites and the Zaydis. The most devout are marked on the forehead by their repeated prostrations.

24   Kawkaban. In theory, each bead of the rosary is meant to invoke one of the ninety-nine attributes of God; in practice it is often no more than a way of passing the time.

25   Shibam. The black turban – originally made of goats' hair – is supposedly the mark of craftsmen and merchants. The wearing of a strip of cloth over the shoulder is a relic of the days before its place was taken by the rifle.

26   Souk al Taleh. In the north, the Maria Theresa silver dollar, called the Rial Franci, is used as currency; as with ammunition, it is often preferred to paper money. Every money-changer in the souk handles such coins every day. In the north, it is the general practice for the men to carry rifles.

27   Sellers of djambias at Sanaa. The value of a dagger depends on the quality of its handle; the finest are made of giraffe's horn, which becomes polished with time to a glowing amber.

28   Young girl at Rawda. The hood, or gargoush, is worn by all babies, and by girls until they are married.

29   Saafan. From an early age, boys take on the responsibility of minding the shop in their father's absence. The kohl around their eyes is a protection against ophthalmia and is also said to ward off the evil eye.

30   Sanaa. The market is flooded with imported goods that provide stiff competition for local products, which are tending to disappear. Aluminium, for example, is replacing stone for dishes and containers.

31   Taez. These painted cases imported from Pakistan and India are often the only furniture in a house.

32   Souk Zabab. The women of Djebel Saber, in the region of Taez, handle all the trade in qat. *The substantial profits have enabled them to exchange their old silver jewellery for new pieces in gold. They are remarkably independent and confident in their manner, and their beauty is legendary. 'They have the advantage of those perfect forms that are to be admired almost nowhere save in those countries where one still is what God has decided one will be.'*★

33   Taez. Dresses are now made of synthetic fabrics from Southeast Asia. The women wear them with trousers. 'For them it is almost in the nature of a religious obligation, for the Prophet declared that God's blessing would be on the women who wore them; which pronouncement he made, when he saw a woman fall over, without suffering any loss of modesty as a result of the accident.' ★ The lower section of the leg is padded as a protection against thorns and prickly bushes.

34   Sanaa. Over the face, the women wear a veil, the mar-moukh; *it is tie-dyed and used to be made of silk, though cotton and nylon are more usual today. The big cloak in which they are enveloped – the* sitara *– is imported from India; it is* put on at puberty and stays with the woman throughout her life, even accompanying her on her bier into the tomb.

35   Souk al Aman. The mark between the girl's eyes represents a tiny palm leaf.

36 and 37   Souk al Khamis, in the north of the Tihama. Crossbreeds are a common sight. Here the nails are painted with khidab (often a manganese compound) in order to emphasize the glow of the skin.

38   Salt deposits at Djebel Djub. The heavy concentration of salt makes it possible to mine blocks of rock salt at certain places on the coast of the Red Sea. On the hill in the background is a Turkish fort.

39   Qanawis. The well is always situated just outside the village; thus it may be used by passing strangers without disturbing the villagers.

40 and 41   Loheya. The arrival and unloading of the sambuks.

42   Crowds at the souk of Al Khamis.

43   Henna on sale at the souk in Tur. The powdered leaves are mixed with water; the women like to add oil to make a preparation for dyeing their hands and feet. The red colour is propitiatory: it symbolizes life and celebration. Old people use it to dye their hair and beards.

44   Mansouria. There are many types of millet, this being a red variety that is among the least nourishing and appetizing.

45   Badjil. These sugared cakes are a favourite delicacy.

46   Woman selling baskets in Mansouria. In the Tihama, a major activity is the weaving of goods such as hats, baskets and netting out of the leaves of the doum palm.

47   This face-painting is done with crushed leaves and is a protection against the sun; it is also meant to make the wearer look ugly and protect her from covetous looks. The silver jewellery is a sign of the family's wealth and of fecundity: with each birth, new pieces are added.

48   Travelling musician at the market in Badjil.

49   Donkeys wait in stone enclosures, while their owners complete their business at the market of Saafan.

50   Dromedary market at Mikhlaf.

51 and 52   Scenes of slaughter. In the country, meat is rarely eaten except on special occasions, and is often sold to bring in money. At the souk you can buy small portions of a mixture of guts, meat and bones all together.

53   Souk Sebt, sales of qat. To retain all its properties, qat should be used as quickly as possible after it is picked.

54   Sanaa. Raisins on sale in the souk. Grown near Sanaa, the grape is regarded as auspicious because it has multiple fruits.

55   Saafan. A discussion about the text of a legal judgment.

56   Badjil. In the Tihama the women have much more freedom than in the high plateaus, and go to the souk unaccompanied.

57   Crowds going to market through fields of qat. Until recently, certain markets and the approaches to them were regarded as places of sanctuary.

58   Crowds milling around the stone huts of Souk Sebt, Saturday's market.

59 and 60   Zagatin. Tur. The dromedary, more common in the Tihama than on the plateaus, is a more delicate animal than the donkey, and less profitable, but it is more prestigious.

61 Bani Awam. Following a path no more than twelve inches wide, the women carry bundles of millet stalks up the mountain; the roots and lower part of the stem are used as fuel, the rest as animal feed.

62 Djebel Milhan. 'As the camels could not go up there, my cases, some of which were very heavy, were brought up by the women of the village, who carried them on their heads; in spite of their burden, they climbed the rocks with an agility that would have done credit to a goat. In the mountains it is always the women who carry the loads, usually on their heads, while the men, on the rare occasions when they stoop to such work, always place their burden on their shoulders.'★

63 and 64 Manakha region. White is the sacred colour and was once used only in the mosques. Pilgrims returning from Mecca sometimes used it to paint designs round their windows. Today it is employed in much the same fashion, but the patterns are highly imaginative and are said to attract light and keep flies away.

65 and 66 There are many fortified villages in Djebel Harraz, where most of the Ismailis live. The community numbers some sixty thousand and maintains close links with India.

67 Village of Bani Awam. The slope of the walls makes the structure of the houses more solid.

★ Taken from an account of a trip to the Yemen, undertaken in 1837 for the Museum of Natural History in Paris by M. Botta, pp. 107, 119.

68 Beit Idhaqa. On the top storey, the mafradj, or reception room, has extensive views. Next to the house is a walled garden of qat trees.

69–72 Meeting of the men from the tribes of Djebel Ashmur to elect representatives of the Co-operative Development Union.

73 Village in the Djawf.

74 Houses at Ibb.

75 House at Sanaa. The windows closed with wooden shutters are in the lower section of the walls of each room, and are there to provide a view; the semicircular glass windows above are a permanent source of light. The little apertures to the side are for ventilation.

76. House at Saafan.

77 and 78 Details of architectural designs.

79 House in the Wadi Bana.

80 House at Radaa; the windows in the lower stories correspond to the stables and the kitchen.

81 Huth. Small boy looking out of his window.

3

4

5

7

8

9

13

14

15

16

18

19

23

24

31

33

36

37

38

43

44

47

54

59

60

72

73

75

76

78

80

81